MAILING MAY

MICHAEL O. TUNNELL

ILLUSTRATED BY

TED RAND

A Tambourine Book

GREENWILLOW BOOKS

An Imprint of HarperCollins*Publishers*

The illustrations were painted in traditional watercolor on 100 percent rag-stock cold-press surface paper.
Mailing May Text copyright © 1997 by Michael O. Tunnell. Illustrations copyright © 1997 by Ted Rand
Manufactured in China. All rights reserved. For information address HarperCollins Children's Books,
a division of HarperCollins Publishers, 195 Broadway, New York, NY 10007. www.harperchildrens.com
Library of Congress Cataloging-in-Publication Data Tunnell, Michael O. Mailing May / Michael O. Tunnell ; illustrated by Ted Rand p. cm.
"A Tambourine Book" Summary: In 1914, because her family cannot afford a train ticket to her grandmother's town,
May gets mailed and rides the mail car on the train to see her grandmother.
ISBN 0-688-12878-5. (trade) — ISBN 0-688-12879-3 (lib.) — ISBN 0-06-443724-8 (pbk.)
[1. Postal service—Fiction.   2. Railroads—Fiction.   3. Grandmothers—Fiction.] I. Rand, Ted, ill. II. Title.
PZ7.T825Mai   1997 [E]—de20 93-35259 CIP AC
❖   16 SCP 30 29 28 27 26 25 24 23 22 21

To Charlotte May
– M.O.T.

With love to Dorothy Kistler,
our family's baby sister.
–T.R.

It all started when Ma and Pa promised I could stay a spell with Grandma Mary, who lived a million miles away through the rough old Idaho mountains. But when I asked Ma if it was time to go, she just shook her head and sighed real deep. So I tried asking Pa.

"No money," said Pa. "Train ticket costs a dollar fifty-five, May. I work all day to make that much. Maybe next year."

But I just couldn't wait a whole year! So the next morning when Ma bundled me in my heavy winter coat and sent me out to play in the snow, I made a beeline for Alexander's Department Store. Mr. Alexander called his hello from atop a ladder.

"I need a job," I said. "I need money for the train."

Mr. Alexander smiled as he stepped down to the floor. "A job, is it? I wish I could hire you, May, but all the jobs around here are grown-up jobs, like counting money and lifting heavy cartons."

I must have looked mighty sad, because Mr. Alexander reached for a jar of peppermint sticks. The sweet, wintry taste didn't do much to cheer me as I slogged my way home.

Things only got worse when Pa came back from work that night. He and Ma commenced to whispering and peeking at me off and on. Then they made me go to bed awful early, which I did not like at all.

Next morning Ma shook me awake while it was still real dark. I was puzzled to see Pa's little traveling bag, packed and standing by the door. When I asked where he was going, Ma only smiled and said, "Eat your breakfast."

Just then someone knocked on our front door. Pa opened up to Ma's cousin Leonard.

"Come along, May," Pa said, grabbing the suitcase as Ma helped me with my coat. "We're going to the post office with Leonard." He held up his hand as I opened my mouth. "No questions," Pa said with a wink.

Ma hugged and kissed me before Pa took my hand and led me out into the dark winter air.

Before long I stood taking in the funny smells of the Grangeville post office: glue and canvas bags and oiled wooden floors. Meanwhile, Pa marched right up to Postmaster Perkins and said, "Sam, you got some new rules for mailing packages. I know boxes can weigh up to fifty pounds nowadays. But what sorts of things can you send?"

Mr. Perkins looked at Pa real strange-like as he asked, "What you got in mind, John?"

"It's May," said Pa. "We'd like to mail her to Lewiston. Leonard here mans the mail car on the train, as you well know. He can take good care of our package."

"Sure thing, Sam," said Leonard.

I was flat flabbergasted by Pa, and so was Mr. Perkins. "Mailing May?" he mumbled, shaking his head.

PARCEL POST

"Let's see. The postal code says not to mail lizards or insects or anything smelly." Mr. Perkins looked at me over his glasses and then sniffed. "Guess you pass the smell test."

"But what about girls?" I asked. "Can you mail me?"

"Well, the rule book says nothing about children, but it is permissible to mail baby chicks." Mr. Perkins smiled. "Let's find out exactly how much you and your valise weigh."

I scrambled up onto the big scale, and Pa set his traveling bag next to me.

"Forty-eight pounds and eight ounces. Biggest baby chick on record!" Mr. Perkins ran his finger down a chart hanging near the scale and turned to Pa. "To mail May from Grangeville to Lewiston will cost fifty-three cents. Well, Leonard, looks like you'll be in charge of some poultry on this mail run."

Before I knew it, Mr. Perkins had glued fifty-three cents' worth of stamps on the back of my coat, along with a label that read:

Mrs. C. G. Vennigerholz
1156 Twelfth Ave.
Lewiston, Idaho

DELIVER TO

Pa hugged me and told me to be good to Grandma Mary. Then he was gone, and there I was, a package sitting in the post office. Before long, Leonard carted me and the rest of the mail to the train station. The big black steam engine was already waiting, hissing and snorting like a boar hog. The sight made me go all tingly, seeing as I'd never ever ridden on a train before.

After Leonard loaded the mail-bags and a few other packages, he called out, "Time to go, May." Then he helped me up the steel steps.

At exactly seven o'clock, the train chugged away from my home and headed down the mountain. I felt as adventure-some as Daniel Boone!

The inside of the mail car was like a little post office, and Leonard got busy right away sorting mail to be dropped off at towns along the way. I curled up nearby the stove to keep warm and watched.

Whenever Leonard had a free minute, he'd take me to the door for a look. My, oh, my, what sights there were to see! Why, we hung on the edge of mountainsides and crawled through tunnels. We crossed deep valleys on top of tall, spidery trestles that Leonard called "steel on stilts."

Then long about Lapwai Canyon, where the train track twists back and forth down the mountain, I began to feel somewhat less adventuresome. Instead, I was feeling dizzy and weak in the stomach. I was about to run to get some fresh air when I heard an angry voice at the door.

"Leonard," yelled a man in a uniform, "that girl better have a ticket or money to buy one."

It was Mr. Harry Morris, the train's conductor. I hid behind Leonard as he explained that I was a package, not a passenger. Then he showed Mr. Morris the stamps on my coat. That cranky old conductor slapped his knee and laughed out loud.

"I've seen everything now," said Mr. Morris, wiping his eyes.

Well, Mr. Morris plumb scared the dizziness right out of me! Even my stomach seemed better, and I started feeling hungry. Leonard said lunch would be at Grandma Mary's.

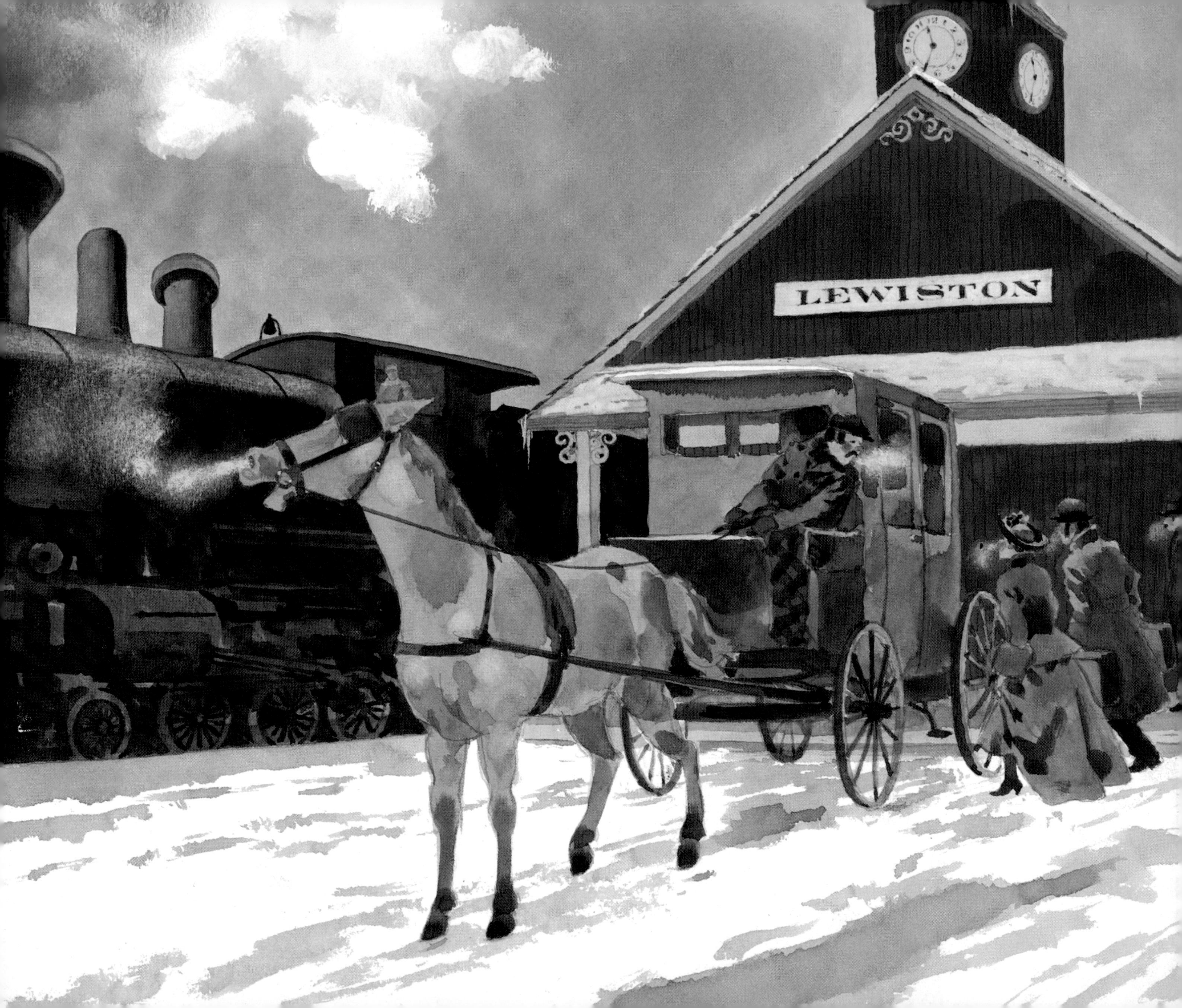
LEWISTON

The train made a few more stops at towns like Sweetwater and Joseph before we pulled into the Lewiston railroad station. Since this was the end of the line, Leonard had time to be my mail carrier, and we headed for Grandma Mary's place.

The second I laid eyes on Grandma
Mary, I felt downright warm inside.
Ma and Pa had kept their promise
after all—with a little help from the
U.S. Post Office!

AUTHOR'S NOTE

This is a true story! On January 1, 1913, the U.S. Post Office Department introduced domestic parcel post service. And on February 19, 1914, five-year-old Charlotte May Pierstorff actually was mailed from Grangeville to Lewiston, Idaho. Indeed, May was classified as a baby chick, and the postage to send her was fifty-three cents. Her mother's cousin, Leonard Mochel, was the railway postal clerk who manned the mail car between Grangeville and Lewiston. Soon after the train arrived, he delivered May to her grandmother.

In those days, there were no decent roads traversing the seventy-five miles of rugged mountain terrain between Grangeville and Lewiston. Traveling by train—either as a passenger or a package—was the only good way to make the trip. And it was difficult to send messages other than by mail or telegraph. Apparently, the decision to mail May came about so quickly that there was no time to notify her grandmother. Or perhaps May's parents wanted to avoid the additional expense of sending a telegram. In any case, Mary Vennigerholz had no idea her granddaughter was coming, much less coming by parcel post.

Though I fictionalized May's story, the basic historical facts are accurate. I learned these facts about May and her incredible adventure from Jim O'Donnell of the National Postal Museum, Lora Feucht of the Nez Perce County (Idaho) Historical Society, Carmelita Spencer of the Bicentennial Historical Museum in Grangeville, Guila Ford and Judith Austin of the Idaho Historical Society, Jim Morefield of the Camas Prairie Railroad (who let me ride the rail between Grangeville and Lewiston), and Gerald Sipes, May's son. Thanks to all of you for your patient assistance. Thanks to Ted Rand for his stunning paintings. And thanks to Leonard Mochel, whose two-page personal account of this story—a clear voice out of the past—solved a number of mysteries for me. I only regret that I missed talking to May herself. She died in 1987.

While chasing May's story, I discovered details about Idaho in the early twentieth century and about postal history, including mail by rail. However, I discovered that the most important detail has nothing to do with railway schedules or postal rates, but rather with the wonderful, creative ways in which ordinary people solve difficult problems.

The illustrator also wishes to acknowledge Dr. Frank Scheer of the Railway Mail Service Library.